Mining the Light

Keith Shein

Copyright © 2015 Keith Shein.

Cover photo by Stephen Dunn.
Author photo by Stephen Dunn.

All rights reserved. No part of this book may be reproduced, stored, or transmitted by any means—whether auditory, graphic, mechanical, or electronic—without written permission of both publisher and author, except in the case of brief excerpts used in critical articles and reviews. Unauthorized reproduction of any part of this work is illegal and is punishable by law.

ISBN: 978-1-4834-2961-8 (sc)
ISBN: 978-1-4834-2960-1 (e)

Because of the dynamic nature of the Internet, any web addresses or links contained in this book may have changed since publication and may no longer be valid. The views expressed in this work are solely those of the author and do not necessarily reflect the views of the publisher, and the publisher hereby disclaims any responsibility for them.

Lulu Publishing Services rev. date: 05/28/2015

AUTHOR'S NOTE

The poem "Blood Sport" appeared in California Fly Fisher. A portion of the poem "Mining the Light" appeared in Field and Stream in a story written by Keith McCafferty. "Cast" was originally published as a broadside by Trike Press.

Many of these poems when first written were dedicated to friends and loved ones. They still are.

This book is for all of you:

Barbara McClure, Bill Morris, Steve Dunn, Carter Cooper, BrendaFlysWithHawks, Keith McCafferty, Bruce Slightom, Jesse McCafferty, Elliott Anderson, Chantelle Cooper, Bill Lowe, Dale Dunn and Marcella Shein

It seemed as if I might next cast my line upward into the air.

—*Thoreau*

CONTENTS

BITS of LIGHT	1
KINGFISHER	2
THE EMBRACE	3
SOUTH COW CREEK ROAD	4
THE SWELLS	6
THE COLOR	7
AWAY	8
MINING the LIGHT	10
INTO the BLACK	11
THE RELEASE	12
BREAKING the SILENCE	13
TWILIGHT	14
CAST	15
GOING HOME	26
TURNING the SURFACE	27
COMES the WIND	28
368	29
HERE WE ARE	30
GRAMMAR	31
OSPREY	32
WATERS	33
TROPICAL	34
DOWN the YENTNA	35
THE LONG HAUL	36
BLOOD SPORT	37
AGAINST the TIDE	39
THE SIXTH	40
CASTING the ASHES	41
ENNIS	42
BLACK and WHITE	43
AH!	44
ARROYO	45
THE PERFECT LOSS	46
THE CLEANING	47
SURE ENOUGH	48
THE MORNING	49
THE ROUNDS	51
BENT to BREAKING	58
SLATE to GREEN	59
OUT of SIGHT	60

SUNDAY BEST	61
FISHING REPORT	62
FLOATING the MORNING	63
NOT FOR NOTHING	64
PIECES	65
THE SMALLEST PEACE	66
TO BE SURE	67
THE CIRCLING	68
INTO the NIGHT	69
BLUE	70
NEW WATER	71
SUN UP	72
THE DEER	73
SOMETHING to CHERISH	74

BITS of LIGHT

We say this with hands because there's no other way.
We say, I reach inside and come up empty.
We're never empty but we can feel that way. The brown
trumpet vine puts out one last purple flower, and we
shake our heads. A breeze shuts our eyes.
Dying camellia blooms litter the sidewalk, and these
can break a heart. We say the heart, but it's not.
It's in our chests, near our hearts, but we don't know what it is.
The blooms look like the tossed corsages from a prom
or flowers from a funeral at sea, though we know nothing's lost
because nothing's kept, even if remembered.
There's a man running his hands over a pond. He seems
to be saying, "It's all right, it's going to be all right,"
and people look but not too long.

I'd like to walk that bridge. I could paint and repaint
the girders and cables so they never rust. I'd live in a shack
down by the water and daily clean my brushes. Because we have
no other way to think about it. Looking out of eyes, there's a gap.
The flight of a hawk lifts us and makes us wonder.
We're not the bird but the bird's in our hearts. We are the bird:
our seeing creates it, in a space that has no wind, no air, where
the bird is not soaring. We can be lonely and lost inside ourselves,
singing to others, the world, not knowing who's calling, who hears.

I'm on a river. Often in my mind I'm on a river. The dark water
swirls around my legs and presses tight. My feet feel
for a hold, then move on, touching, floating for another hold.
Railroad trestles stand fallen in the stream, and spent mayflies
cloud above the water. They shine as if they've swallowed
bits of light, and the weight floats them down. When the fish strikes,
my heart races, but that's not what brings me to the water.
There's a hollow moment when the fish darts, pulling to get free.
When I release the fish, it feels like I'm holding my own emptiness.
When it fins away, I'm not any fuller or free, but I breathe, then, the river.

KINGFISHER

A truck rattles by, rumbling.
Bird song follows, and it feels like it might rain.

Then a kingfisher, solitary as always, lights
on a snag in the river, just the two of us

with the water between. The bird seems a sign,
but so did the path that tangled in scrub.

I could hear sound of the river through the branches—
its smell like sour tea. Going back

up, then, to go round, only to stumble down
the nettled bank, and the path right there

in the trees. Or the breath of wind caught in leaves,
or a stone, the one colored one side

like a mask and the other like a heart, cold,
warming to the touch, but mute

as things can be. Clouds, wind, the casts draw lines
in the water, reach, disappear, swing

and come up empty, the top the same as the bottom.
When I look up from untangling a knot, the kingfisher

has flown. But I know things I could not know,
and cast and cast again.

The line comes: if what we eat becomes us,
what we crave are ghosts. The line comes tight.

The fish gasps on the beach, but that's not what
turns me wild. It was the bird—believing the bird.

THE EMBRACE

The green limbs of a living neighbor
hold the redwood, its brown tip curled.
The dead redwood stands.

But not held. Hung up. Caught.
And not standing—only not fallen.
To see this is to see the truth.
And to fail.

The tip turned just so, the tender bend.
But not tender.
Fog hanging at the ridge top.
                              Like what?
Like a bone mist, like a cape of breath,
the white we want to see
when on our knees, helpless.

I bend to the river and reach my hands
as if to warm them in the gleams.
Humility is a harsh teacher. I try to see
the greatness in the pebble as well
as the peak, and I can't. But I am here, bowed
in the woods, a whisper in the wilderness,
breathing in, breathing out. When I stand,
I'm fallen. When I sway, I'm held.

SOUTH COW CREEK ROAD

I first heard wind
but it was really the drone of flies.
What I would have liked to see
was the skid when your spirit arced the flesh—
but I'm sure it was blinding.

There's a word for this, the calm
that comes from a closed body of water.
The surface lies flat.
Black mayflies hatch out of the lake
and trout suck them back down.

Perhaps you felt something like this,
draining into a vortex, slowly
as the life left, then fast as it twisted
into another shape or none, kept spinning.

There's a guy wearing shiny loafers, sitting on his tackle box.
He's got on gray dress slacks and brown suspenders
over his gray-striped shirt. Currently, his fedora is off
while he works on his bobber.

There's no name for this—if you say it out loud.
Because of the tightness in the throat,
if you say it out loud it sounds like bleating.
A bald eagle flies over the lake.
With each pass, the wild swans on the water
flutter and rise in a frightened white cloud,
settle when it takes a perch.

I keep thinking you weren't ready
and you panicked—
in a second you had no skin or weight,
were boundless, swimming without a breath,
or peeling light and grabbed the first free form.
How could you know the way?

From here, there's an end beginning. I can see
the peace from nature comes not from its beauty but scale.
There's the white flank of Mt. Lassen reflected,
a damsel fly settling on its watery peak.
The old man has caught a fish and turned up the brim of his hat.

Leaving, I pass Long Hay Flat Road and Brokeoff Meadow,
places passed before, though before,
when you were alive, I never thought to mention them to you,
and now it's too late for a difference.
The sign says Fresh Eggs, Pigs and Cut Flowers.

THE SWELLS

The white specs on the swells are boats, all named Desire.
For moments they roll out of view, and we progress

until the next wave lifts, and the boats take shape,
bear down, and we too are white on their horizon,

blue miles we scratch, cast after cast, touching nothing.
The motor drones and the propeller keeps churning.

Overhead, the sun burns the air and its wheeling birds.
Whatever course we plotted is now a wandering,

heated, though only by hours. But at last we raise a fish,
huge, bronze-headed. It slices toward the boat, sail arched,

bill slashing, enraged iridescence lighting its sides.
It rises on its tail, thrashes in air, dives and is gone.

The line goes slack and sinks lazily below the foam, the rod
straight though the man holding it still stoops with the struggle,

hands quivering, sweat dripping off the bill of his cap.
The swells grow larger, lifting the bow, our eyes

to the sky as if searching for the light's edge, all
we can hope for, white as a handkerchief on the waves.

THE COLOR

We're parked on the roadside, looking at color,
and we're not alone.
There's an RV, a pickup, a jeep.
Pocket cameras click, video cameras pan.

Down the ravines, yellow aspen stream,
and on the flanks,
they're an orange-yellow ripple.
It takes the breath away.

We can't help it.
Here's the annual pageant of trees
and we hit the brakes to swerve into a pullout
and gawk.

But it's not respect, even awe,
though our eyes widen. And it's not that
this is our first fall, not by a long shot.
It's the vista,

this side of the canyon dropping hundreds
of feet to the valley, darkening, deep.
Then up the far side, the peaks white
year-long, the range stretching

until the color blurs into haze,
the land's hue merging with the sky's,
an ocher mist at vision's limit.
We try to take it in.

It's not the least bit heroic. It has no motive
in beauty. The beauty pounds down on us, huge,
bountifully, until we're thoughtless, small
as our breath, aware of each other's breath.

AWAY

The moon is a bright bite.
One by one the cabins in the pasture
turn on their lights and become
light boxed.

The moon is a bright bite.
Patience, it takes patience
to see the dark, which
has its own shades, and stars.

Now the snow gleams blue,
and on the highway, white lights
mix with red, and sound
like the sea.

What I'm thinking
is that love turns cold
and back, day in, out.
In an hour you can hear the night

where you are. Then comes
dawn, and at the mountain's foot,
fog shimmers.
What I thought didn't matter.

Distance fits tight as skin.
Why is it that we remember
agony, like a place?
I went to the Agonies.

I caught some fish.
The stream curves and mirrors
its slice of sky, while in the mist,
mayflies hover like ghosts.

Just as easily we might remember
pleasure, nights next to the bakery
when we were up late enough
to laugh and beat on the walls

as they rattled the pans.
Miles hold silence like a cup.
Somehow the sage smells cold,
and what we captured was ourselves

tying fear to love because
we touched loss. There
should be scars but there aren't.
The stream cuts the pasture

with patient bends,
and the tossed rock vanishes.
What I hope is that
we might take our clothes off

in the absolute dark
of a strange room, and one
by one turn the lights on
and look very closely

at all that we can see.
If you're still, you can stand
on the bank and watch the dark
eat the ribbon of water

all the way to your feet.
There's a distance
that lives
just in our thoughts.

The moon is a bright bite.
What called in the day
falls silent, and the night
casts shade for the stars.

MINING the LIGHT

What's silver on shore does not light the deep,
at least what I can see, peering into the river.
Mining for light. Caught full in the bright of day,
searching with a hook.

They're swimming upstream, the green water
dark over their backs, black as it swirls
over the bed, deepening in the pools.
I imagine them glowing down below, each a lantern
to the next as they find their way against the current.

Against the odds.
Five hundred miles from sea and some still chrome,
some with their rainbows returning,
all strong with the pulse of life, the urge to spawn,
in the penumbra of the hunted.

What I can't see, I feel, the line taut, the line
like a nerve reaching down.
Beneath the surface, there's a flash
when the fish shows its side,
the light that blinds.

Now there's nothing to be seen except this brightness,
sinking. Three times I haul the fish to my feet,
three times I see the light slip back to the black.
It would seem as if I struggle against a weight, back bent,
head back, boots dug in stones.

But there's no measure for how heavy light is,
what strength it takes to lift the river's flame
to the light of day, how bittersweet to see the fish
on the bank, brighter than the simple sun.

INTO the BLACK

At home, the silk trees bloom, red as embers in summer's air.
In my mind, they light the way to things known,
all that ties to place.

Here, the river takes the last light and leaves a flowing ink.
Here, I can say, if only a whisper,
My heart is dark, dark.

Gray doves, out of gray sky, whistle into the trees;
the cliffs, which held the light, flatten,
and, as blacker patches, bats flicker.

I wade into the black.
The current wraps around me.
My hands burn as I dip them in the river.

What is it we cannot know but need to draw near?
The river sings louder in the night, as if set free.

It feels as if reaching for silence into a silence too large to keep,
a distance tight as a ring, where I can seek, where I will not
stop seeking.

In the dark, nothing's claimed, not even faith.
Dark, dark, I whisper, and the line comes tight,
the fish so gold, it warms.

I slip it back into the black, and follow.
Deeper, I cast and cast again.
My heart is dark, I say. Pray the light sees.

THE RELEASE

To spawn, the steelhead survive a gauntlet of sea lions
at the river mouth, climb five dams, swim upstream
hundreds of miles to the exact place of their nascence.

I want to touch that liquid summons.

Yet when the line between us shivers, I feel alone,
the fish dancing on the river, running with the current
back downstream, and me backing toward shore.

I remove the hook and lift her, marveling at her silver sides,
her great length and strength brought to rest on the bank.
She's spent, held out of the water, quiet in my grasp.
When put back in the stream, cradled against the current,
she keeps in my hands, finning before swimming away.

It's like a man to wound what he loves.
Clouds hang in the trees.

BREAKING the SILENCE

At the river's edge, I'm speaking my mind,
or my heart, I'm not sure the difference,

but talking to the water, offering thanks,
saying goodbye,

in love with it, the way a child marvels at something
large and wild.

At a quiet eddy, I stand, holding
my palms out, bringing a fist to my chest,

wishing the river and fish stay strong, healthy.
You see what I mean—

hoping that the river hears.
But I say it anyway, right into the roaring air.

Stumbling, because it's like a prayer but isn't,
stuttering, because I'm standing in sagebrush talking

to a stream. Still, the words come and then stop when
I've said my bit. A stillness then almost like silence.

I can close my eyes and see the riffle running down
to the bridge, the shining heads of trout rising.

I can be anywhere, close my eyes, and hear
the currents' sighs.

In the quiet, a fish rises, sending a ring
toward the bank, one circle.

I stand watching the ring disappear. I walk away
on two legs, same as I came. But nearly at peace.

TWILIGHT

There's a way the garden is the prairie and the mountain is the house.
The eyes see a rose and a river, the hand feels for the door handle,
hawk or heart—the birds that live with us, the windows, fish.
Outside, rivers and mountains, freeways, chairs. The land is a street
and the boat floating. The great elk laid down in the meadow,
the rumpled bed where we sleep, tractors and hay bales, the pools
with trout rising, the dark bars, doublewides, the blank eyes
of the ranchers who've seen it all.
We all get back to nature on vacation.
We need to get to work,
hearing the water's clock, slowing the steps, cautious into the stream.
The dark like a waterfall tumbling, the light like a lake.
If we take that turn, I think we'll find it.
We're lost, admit it, no streetlights, address, the trees bent in twilit winds,
pine trees and burnt trees black as coal, fire that jumped the river,
lives drowned, our own, broken sheds, plastic geese in a V
nailed to the barn, the two-tracks leading god knows where.
Turning the radio dial to find a music that matches the dark,
a distance that might diminish, a dance with our partners in all the lit houses
we pass as we go, because we must keep driving.

CAST

1
Looking out from the rest stop,
we learn: Nevada's Humboldt River
had to be discovered. Trouble
with the name though—Unknown,
Perry, Squaw—for Ogden's
ignorance of where it went,
his dying guide, the bride
of his next compadre. Indians
got one in too, Humpneck
or some such. Propane
Laundry. Draw an equal between
the boondocks and huge satellite dishes,
undoing the symmetry of the shacks.
Cows chew around a field's
only thing. Question is,
have I ever used the tent?
I hold her _____
fetched from inside it in reply.
Otherwise, I remember Montana.
That I'm here without her
causes a pain as if made
by a crude surgical tool.

2
Hooked three times to the same
fight downstream, up the river's middle
to a channel too deep to wade:
bust it off or go in—or hand the rod off,
he thought, to someone on shore:
tag team fishing.
In Last Chance it reads Laundr*o*mat
on the roof and Laundr*a*mat on the sides,
over the old bar's yet legible name.
Sports, in sporting hats and pipes,
whipping the water in style.
Wading Box Canyon, half the body
in the raging current, cold and afraid.

Coming out of the Grizzly Bar,
equal parts story and air. Simply,
the fish focus on food, a place
to hold, hide, from the birds above,
other fish, "you," the pronoun
that shifts between the human
and the rest. The moon, home,
equally far away.

3
Deluge, gully washer, each
rippling shade of the river
impenetrable, floating skill
to hope—as with a face.
The more it seems skin,
the less it has complexion,
the more eyes "pool."
At the thought, not the thunder.
When the sky cracks, that thing
between calm and fear runs
to the car. Cast the line.
The strike vibrates with a kind
of terror, rising to a conclusion
unknown. With more and more
difficulty, I recall the mannerisms
that passed for knowledge of her.
The pleasure so sure a thing.
No pleasure in a thing.
Frantic at the thought
of the keys lost, searching
the bags again and again,
certain they're there, knowing
they're not, smiling at the mystery
solved: in the ignition.

4
Dry landscape, empty of green,
radio waves gathered
from all the West, the progress

alien, movie-like, imagination
so drenched in *versions* of space.
Which is greater, the loss
of home, family, sense?
Shooting stars probably rip
any night whose sky has stars
to see. Thought makes
the head a globe the world
can't enter. He says,
People ought to be forced
to look at the sky, ask questions.
I take notes with the idea
of passing the knowledge
to my son—seized by images
of his small body swept away
by the current. I will tie him
to me, I cannot tie him to me.
Strange as it seems, the *country*
places government apart from
the people. Where did they
come from, how do they live
here? When the rod cracked,
it was like a small caliber shot.

5
Whiskey sharpened his tongue,
to wit, Sport Evolution:
the lower rung, ourselves,
spilled out cars to sleep on dirt;
the higher ups ensconced
in bright Winnebagos;
at the top, with guides,
sipping cocktails in lodges.
Lower Sport Stew: when chopping
onion to freshen canned beans,
whack a hunk off thumb. His heart
seizes, or so he thinks,
but feels where he is,
wading a river, miles from help.
Put some men near water, a glaze
transforms their eyes. In town,

metal elks graze around the bank.
The other bank changes one day
to the next, there to be stepped on,
stepped on, gives.
Saved by a staff, a phone call.
He says a week after the baby came,
he was back fishing. Everything,
permission itself, testimony to her.
She's not behind him, anywhere,
but where she is. She says, A man
can come inside her, nine months later
help with the birth, look in her eyes
and not know what she feels.
Okay, go. He takes her word for it.
Videos and Chainsaws Sharpened Here.

6
Underground, forces shoved
mountains east-west, putting at odds
what one thought: water flows
south but not here. Lightning
is explained. The DJ stutters
a warning. The outhouse runs
out of tp. Tuesday,
the underwater crew will explore
what turns the switch on fish,
one moment making the river boil,
the next dead calm. They find
a forest of fishing poles, no fish.
First drop of rain lands
right in the eye of the hook.
The inscrutable surface clears,
lightning veers and, tottering,
one balances will and that other.
Pliers don't seem so, but when
the hook's deep in, they're gentlest.
Dunked. Chilled to the bone
in the aquarium of my clothes.

7
Looking back, the assumption was
that love should come naturally.
It didn't, sickened, died—
something we didn't know
how to fix. With the mind or something.
Her face not unlike the moon's,
that far, that faceless. Travel
Nevada at night. You can get lucky,
have a good car, but can't help feeling
increasingly small rounding another
curve to another endless straightaway.
The state spares no expense
for this rest stop: Xed 4x4's
holding up tin roofs. Then,
the moment the tackle ceases to feel
clumsy, divorced from what's at hand.
The good ones will talk about
knowing when the fish strikes,
mystifying the mystery.
The fly thirty feet away, seen, then lost,
fish *on,* writhing, uncertain
what's to come. I say,
It's just like life, ironically,
to get a laugh. Doesn't get a laugh.
One year: the mayfly
lives 364 days under water, hatches,
flies, mates, dies—in 1 day.

8
Question is, if you saw the face
in time, could see past
the banged-up satchel, filthy
pants, if there were room, if the face
were your own, would you know it,
give yourself a ride?
Because the rain comes, the flies
hatch, the fish take them.
Seeing the horse with its plastic
legs raised, rotating for its ad,
the rows of women 8 AM, hunched,

tying flies over vices, I feel I know
where I am. Because I've seen it
before. True and not.
The entire state in drought.
Doesn't matter that it's rained
every day since arriving,
a perspective so local it's lame.
I keep coming back.
Inevitably, when I write as I drive
I go faster. In the photo
of the big one, it looks like
I'm trying to strangle its every inch—
releasing it.

9
Left, left, turn left, you idiot,
we've already *had* that experience.
Beer me. Nothing happening.
One on a wet fly, one hooked
pulling in line to untangle
a knot. Catalogue of things lost:
one rod, reel, flies, fly box,
knife, camp chairs, lantern, grill.
Big fish—as many as five at your feet,
nibbling nymphs as you wade.
Doing our job, whipping the water,
waiting—with a retrieve,
a dead drift. Use a belt:
waders filled with water
have drowned even the strongest
swimmers. Where's my belt?
The whole world wet—hot pots
steaming, backs of fish rolling out
into rain to take dime-sized duns.
Flies fear fish, fish fear birds,
rain hides both, it was his third
maybe his fourth run,
biggest so far. A slicker cuff
nicks the reel, and snap, he's off.
That was the day. It was a bitch.
Sitting on the bank, looking

more and more bored the more
into it he got.

10
We sit in camp chairs, middle
of the motel room, switching the TV's
blurry channels, thumb on
the remote control. The faster
the image, the more frozen the fix.
Sit in front of crackling fire,
chin in hand, pondering the twitch
of flame. Sit steering the spent
chassis, each curve dictating
station change, punch of any button,
thereby stay sane. Local radio
a peepshow onto other lives.
Rip it off, rip it all off.
Reach out, scrape away an aspen
grove, a gas station. A shaggy dark
settles on a mountain peak,
river churning at its base.
What weighs are the scratches
of stars. Make it dance, make
the wood burn down to nothing,
sit a man in reach. He'll stare,
fit another piece into the logic
and watch it burn.

11
Did we make it here?
Blasting across the desert.
No, limping. The radiator
leaking by Reno, hairline
crack at the neck. Astonished
to see the Keno addicts
chipper and at it so early.
Which of us smashed the rod
in the car door, the hatch so thick
our hands had to find the river?

Doesn't matter. It seems you
are history by then, reduced.
Funny though, not till I got home,
laid the tent out to air, that
I found _____ *again*.
Only to create the illusion of will
do they put arms on the slots, then
hand out wipes to clean the grime
from fingering money. Stranded,
a bill for solder hurts. Who do I pay?
I ask. Who do you owe?

12
Such a male world, for no
clear reason. She gets the fish
within ten feet of shore
and lets her dog splash after it,
and if it's a whitefish, keeps
throwing it back for the dog.
So easy to be cruel to a sucker,
three vicious shakes on the line,
then limp. Inevitably, when the miles
grind, we talk about relationships.
It isn't the hours. His eyes
dart, knowing exactly the threat,
his life long tangled with hers,
failing, but obscurely. Truth is,
I don't know the sex
until the blade splits the belly.
We always refer to them as he.
He busted me off. He was
a mother.

13
Bloodies his thumb when he grabs it
by the jaw. Pulls the gills through
its mouth trying to get the hook out.
And because we mostly let them go,
forgets to kill dinner. Beans again,

dogs. Bison. The tourists get within
ten feet of the rutting beasts, get gored.
Jealous of the family at the roadside, he,
sway-backed, slack-bellied, dumb tattoo
on shoulder, she, in cut-offs, lifting
her heavy thigh over his, embracing
on the shred of grass. The babies
playing in a puddle, rusted van hulking
in the lot. What must it feel like
to be lifted out of the stream, breaking
the film that means breath,
though it keeps working its gills,
trying, drained from the fight—
as if tame as I revive it, moving it
back and forth in the stream, only to
watch it sink, motionless, out of sight.
Sickening. Attempting an image,
the story offered fishing's stalk
as the progress of love. What
unforgivable drivel.

14
His mind wasn't in his dream yet,
the murderer said, asked in court
why it took so long to move
with his son into the wild.
The chain used to hold
the kidnapped woman buried
eight years in wait.
On bicycle for god's sake,
itinerant crazies, as if plucked
from some inner city and plopped,
peddling in the void. JESUS
SAVES painted large on the trailer.
Braced sideways to lessen the current,
holding until the hole's exhausted
or hopeless, wanting to
make it back to the bank.
One foot up and you're gone,
touching again ten feet
further downstream, floating out

of control. So the fish
hold predictably, behind rocks,
where fast water swirls food
by the slow, and not too much
energy's lost facing upstream.
The cost of it. Protein versus
the draw of a continent. Memory
versus liquor in the blood.
The entire Milky Way in sight.
Versus grief. I look out
at the light-stippled water,
the constant changing image.
Frozen, look out.

15
The reel sings. Blue moon.
You can be sighting the Big Dipper,
from it the North Star, hearing a story
when northern lights appeared,
and realize a cliché has astronomical fact:
full moon, twice in one month. Once
in every _____. Which fact is heard
but not registered. I _____ you.
Inevitably too soon or late. Should've
been here last week, hadda beat em off
the hook. No, you're a little early
for hoppers, _____ is when them
hoppers come. Facts grow
the longer they live in the mind.
I watch those times become a thing.
Drunk, flat on our backs in the weeds,
thinking we'd be better able to read
the star map that way. A ghost,
like the Little Dipper. I'm told
if the northern lights appear
so must the southern. It can be
August, is, hotter than hell.
You can be sipping a cold one,
sweating in some bar—you know
what the locals are talking about?
Winter, or snakes.

16
Seems like home but echoes.
The rod bends. The bird hits
the car antennae. Bless clouds.
I have a vision of a woman
coming down from the sky
with brown exacting eyes.
Can you believe such imagining?
Sometimes just not being able
to turn around creates a future.
We're lost, and the dirt two-track
vanishes, as this high desert
and blue water don't seem to fit,
which cannot be. She puts
the deer skull up for a mask.
The town has a name but no place.
Maybe this time, this one.
I look up at the sky, shout,
It could be cooler—but this is
too personal. When she lands,
I hold her so close the buttons hurt.
The Christians pray at the roadside,
in the rain. I've got her wading
in the river, thunder all around,
and the rod sparks. We pour
over the map and can't refold it.
When we stop for the night,
Twin Falls.

GOING HOME

Sudden thunder shakes the ground,
rain lashing the prairie.

In an hour, the sage will smell damp,
fertile, blue sky will scrub through

black clouds. But as we dry, the lightning
lives in us, as the birds begin

to wildly sing, we try to remember how
we survive when the heart catches fire,

then cools, when we're trembling
then wishing we trembled more.

Up in the air, the tall trees already look
stunted; the river of our dreams weaves

through smudges of hills,
and we're wondering on which island

the bear lives, his growls echoing,
the wolf howls thinning to whispers.

In our pockets, the bright coins made
of sparks, but we're not sure, going home,

we've saved enough for the daily toll,
flying, as if we knew how, the mountains

already fading to plains, the sameness.
Hoping the bags arrive, the flames.

TURNING the SURFACE

The river's been at it, polishing sharp edges,
clouding the glass, but Log Cabin reads clear,
as is the outline of the little shack, and *Syrup*.

I keep an eye out while following the river,
the odd rock or shell, bits of bone.
I take them home and put them on a shelf
or sill, this wilderness.

To remember those places, these shards.
Trying to keep the man I am behind a desk
the man I am by the water.
Fingering the things. Collecting.
Forgetting. Leaking through my grasp.

COMES the WIND

On the green mountain, one tree shapes
a yellow plume, small in the scale
but brighter because of it, and later,

when up the valley fall's color burns,
it will seem lit by this spark,
flickering until the hillside rages.

Faces as ovals of light shining on the banks,
lined-up as if beacons for the boats,
the salmon and steelhead swimming the dark.

The river's colors shifting, blue from
a height as it takes in the sky, green,
black. From some distances, even near,

we appear to be growing out the stream,
anchored to our reflections.
Then comes the wind.

368

Where the trees stand along the bank, wind breaks,
bowing the branches then moving on.
On the sawed pole a number, 368,
to mark this place for the train,
our camp along the river.

The current wraps our legs.
We take shape in it, step down another shape.
There's mystery here, under the moving skin.
We send a line out, bring it back. We gather air.

After a time, it seems almost possible to cast
without a line, as if the gesture were all,
and reeling fish to hand was not the end
nor the mystery, that we might make it
come to us.

Bright lights of the stream.
The cottonwoods' fluff floats down
and melts in the riffle.
You can follow the railroad tracks to just this spot.
You'll see the pines and the river-bend, a canary
in the willows, head cocked.

I'm that man half-lost under the water,
feet feeling for a hold.
The other half might be anyone.
When you find this place, you'll see how disappeared
I am, down the ceaseless underneath.

HERE WE ARE

There's a waterfall at the trail's end, rainbows
splashed out the pool. Here we are,
looking out over a precipice, posing,
hoping the colors come through.

All those photos tucked away,
taped, forgotten. There we were,
not looking what we look like, younger,
gathered on a river bank. We appear

happy to have arrived, perhaps just smiling
for the camera. Turning the pages,
looking back as down a tunnel
at what we may have felt then: hero

shots, the tarpon from the Keys, striper
from SF Bay, the Klamath steelhead,
Alaska salmon, trout after trout
after trout.

Clicking the shutter, filling the album.
Keeping what fades bright for memory.
Here, some recent ones not yet taped in place.
We almost look like we look. Again, smiling.

GRAMMAR

On the wire, dawn's hawk sits,
fat as a comma,

one line of meaning coming, caught
in its claws, another leaving,

as the first light fills around
the stars.

OSPREY

Wings knifed
to dive

the swooping
hawk

cuts through
fog

smoothed
by its tail

WATERS

Water, different waters,
wind swept or still, roiling with current,
catching shadows out a shimmering
yet to give back himself, which takes sight into itself,
more liquid than the eye.

In the north, clouds bud, and from low on the horizon,
scraps gather and move. The mind too transforms,
wringing thought out of sense while what's constant
is the tide piling up then retreating from shore.

Out of silence comes quiet, a watching as do the cormorants
in the trees, each seeing a different melting ghost.
Now the wind shuffles out of the west, and the focus
narrows to a few yards of nervous water.

He sees the line tighten as it hisses in the film,
the gray body turn silver shining in air.
He sees nothing more until his hands dip into the sea,
releasing what can't be kept, the clouds black over the palms
along the beach, the separate winds weaving.

Now, it's my turn to take the bow and stare, blood running,
trying to see out the water gleams take shape.
Past the roots of the mangroves, the man with the pole
pushes us on.

TROPICAL

When I'm a wave, I wash upon the rocks
against the hard edges that shape me,
wearing stone to sand.

When I'm the electric light on the pier,
shining through night into morning,
I'm most human, that land's end
keeps a brightness.

And when I'm the bonefish
in the shallow flats, swimming ghostlike over sand,
with scales like mirrors,
with a sad and expectant face,
I'm most myself, for reasons only the water
can say, and the water only murmurs and roars.

There's a man casting into the turquoise,
as if writing the story of himself, the lines
erased as soon as they're written,
as soon as they're erased, written again.

DOWN the YENTNA

The river brown, roiled with glacier melt scoured
from the mountains and running to the sea,
and into that churn, a green stream swirls.

The salmon smell it and turn toward their birth,
females fat with eggs, males turning red,
jaws hooked to spawn.

Ahead of them, the kings have come,
their loose eggs rolling backwards as down a hill,
their huge bodies showing up dead in the shallows,

haunting. Now the sockeye swim past,
silent, fecund, fish after fish. Bear tracks in the mud,
eagles in the trees, a family of foxes trotting the bank.

I'm knee-deep in the river, thinking of how far
one must travel to see something so exotic, when
it's nothing of the kind. I have not loved life enough.

THE LONG HAUL

And if the water offers its gift,
silver fish after fish, purple glazing their sides,
a blessing this day when so many
come up empty?

I pray, leaving a sprinkle of tobacco on the water,
but what can I say?

It's not lucky. What's luck, I think,
but wishing done, and I'm hungry, hungry
to be back on the water as soon as my foot
touches shore, and what should I say?

At the dock, filled with wonder,
with thanks to its spirit, I kill the one fish kept,
but say not a thing.

I wash the boat, coil the lines,
break down the rod. Look back
at the water still holding my gaze, to the land
which keeps me.

I'm talking out loud but to no one.
Or the words are for myself. OK, I say, OK,
starting the truck for the long haul home.

BLOOD SPORT

She wonders why anyone
who loves fish would hurt them,
hooked to be released.
I'm older, and she knows
there's blood on my hands.

I hold up my hands,
each one held by another man
and another in turn to make a ring
around the rivers we love.
Bloody, she says, regardless.

She's young, angry and right.
If I were young, I'd take her hand
and walk down to the river,
show her the stream the way a fisher
sees it, the pools, the cut banks

where the trout hold, the seams
where fast water meets the slow.
Tell her about the last hour
before dark, the clouds
of caddis hatching, the silence

of ten thousand wings, the wade
into the river, the current's pull,
casting, reaching, the connection
when the line comes tight—
and trust my heart to that ardor.

But I'm silent and look away.
To the river which owns my heart,
to the hope that when I go down
trout will be rising,
that each hour on the water

shapes a better man, in love
with creation, waist deep in it, thirsty
for the wild, its mystery, who can do
more than look at his hands.
A better man will know what to say.

AGAINST the TIDE

The wind comes up against the tide,
and the water rears, breaking
over the rails.

I throttle down and ease back
toward port, picking my way
through the roil to safe harbor.

The boat should have a name, I think,
I should be calling out her name now
instead of talking to myself, the spray

stinging, dark sky crashing
the horizon, lightning, then thunder
shuddering the hull.

I think, it's no time
to be thinking of this, except this
seems the time of such thinking.

The bow plows under and bounces up,
shoveling water over the gunwales.
A woman's name, or Osprey, Orion,

perhaps a fish, but not nameless—
the nameless claims me, gripping
the slippery wheel.

THE SIXTH

The sixth man on the raft is a wraith, but he weighs.
The dead are heavy, though we float, and the cliffs rise

above the river, trees on their crests, looking exactly
like the world

but black, when what we wanted was a ribbon
of endless green and the quiet return of the eddies.

One builds a fire, another pitches the tents, one sets
the chairs on the bank as we go about the tasks of camp.

The sixth chair, we didn't bring.
We're quiet, though we have around us the freedom of the woods,

tired, though we have nothing which seems like work.
We have each other, but not close.

The river calls and I walk down to it. Odd
to take a place near the water and not want something out of it.

I tell myself: sit, for once just goddamn sit.
I fidget.

What we fear is the far and dark made near.
All of us yet see his face. The sixth man hovers.

CASTING the ASHES

Life is rich, he said, though life bred the demons
that took his life, and he rode them hard.
Life is rich, even as the cancer ate him, rich, even
as he died, haunting family and friends.

At the campsite where he last staked a tent among ours,
we bring his ashes. Everywhere we look
is his absence, in the dust on the stones, the wind listless
in the branches, in the tattered sky; and everywhere we look,
the world turns green, in the grasses over the hills, the wild iris
on the river bank, in the sadness, ripening.

His urn is a Budweiser can, sawed open at the top. That's not him,
we say. But it's him. And fitting that in the place we fished,
they now spawn. All day, they're at it, the striped males swarming
the hens, clouding the water with milt. All day and into night.
And in the morning, they're still there, holding in the shallows.
Casted out, his ashes make a momentary plume, swept away.
We say not a word.

On an old board, we carve Life Is Rich.
Then, one by one, each takes a letter and, with a tool, burns it black.
The wood is gray, nearly weightless from decades outdoors,
yet burned, each letter oozes sap, the pine scent unmistakable,
resin smoldering, the smoke smelling like the campfires he lit,
our architect of flames. Sap, after all these years.
Life Is Rich.

In the dark, I keep casting, hoping for one more fish.
With each flick of the rod, the bats draw near;
as the line hisses out, they follow. I cast and cast
but come up empty.

ENNIS

Small town:

the blue mortuary
is for lease.

BLACK and WHITE

Like a magpie
on a dead skunk.

AH!

Now, I can see
the fish,

wriggled free
of flesh,

skin a peeled
wrinkle,

its bleached
bones gleam.

ARROYO

In summer I sit
on the hot dry stones
where water flows in winter.
The wind is an echo,

dust in the hollows,
I walk the bed.
Then, in my skin,
I am the stream

running between banks.
I'll wait until fall.
My friend, the water,
is more than a ghost,

a dove, softly,
I whistle, a whisper,
a trickle, like the last
spring rain.

THE PERFECT LOSS

The sun low, and quiet at camp,
all resting in hammocks
or sitting in shade, not speaking, beat.

Morning, afternoon spent
reading the river, wading,
searching, casting, watching,
hours without thought—

not of home, family, failure
or regret, not the daily diminishments,
not the deaths, nothing of the voices
that haunt—

but lost in the churn of the water,
until only the roars and ripples
are heard, nothing
but the press of the current

and the slippery stones, spires
of pines, quarrels of warblers, fish,
crimson in hand—

and the hunt, stalking the stream
for the next foam line,
pool, cut bank, the next riffle—

and then the hike back to camp,
to the world of glances, ourselves,
eyes closed, resting quietly in the shade—

until we stand as if stumbling
out a dream—already thinking
of evening, the return to the river,
the perfect loss.

THE CLEANING

The underside's pearl,
so that when it rises to feed,
from below, it seems another
piece of the brightening.

When the blade enters
and slices toward the head,
there's a red gash from tail
to jaw, and the guts spill
into the river.

Now meat, its rainbow fades,
and slipped into the bag,
it curls, stiffens, the water
from its rinsing blushed with blood.

Cooked with their heads on,
the black eyes are their most
disquieting, open and dull.
But the first bite closes our eyes;
our heads tilt back.

After, the bare bones
look somehow like keys
on the plates. We feed them
to the fire.

In the morning, we leave the pit
covered with dirt, pour water
over the yet hot coals, hunger
troubling the belly again.

SURE ENOUGH

From afar, as we drift downstream, it looks like a tree
with roosting birds, the branches bare but filled
with different colors, one of those scenes where different species
perch in peace, living off the river. Pretty fecund and cool.

No, he says, those are shoes.
I squint, and sure enough, floating by, I make out
the laces, uppers and soles. Damn kids, he sighs. Look,
there's even a bra.

No doubt, it's reckless, littering,
but it's human, too, and I grin. I can see
the shoes flung up to beery shouts, the bra thrown to cheers
and pumped fists, the drunken flotilla of sunburned kids
sprawled on inner tubes, laughing and floating on.

Above us on the cliffs, mansions hover.
The bank rises high and sheer, and the river eats it, rains
wear it away. We can see recent slides, muddy on the bank,
and higher, retaining walls and aprons of concrete.
From the rear decks, at the cliff edge, there must be beautiful views.
This, too, is human. But I look away to the dark mirror of water.
Some part of me hopes it all crashes down.

THE MORNING

Now the robin chirps over his seed,
and she thinks he'd eat more but for that crowing.
It's morning. Another robin hops on the feeder,
and an argument grows.

She weeps,
her husband hears her.

Some slopes of the mountains grow no trees,
and from here in the valley, the green faces seem smooth,
curve as they descend as some lines of the body
that his hand gently follows down her arm.

She doesn't turn.

Her eyes move, the eyes are not satisfied at rest, and wander now
along the ridge to a peak, then down. She sees
fog stand like twisting wraiths on the river, and the canyon's trees
so darkly green they purple.

She hears the door shut.
He hears it the other side.

Swallows swoop around him as if whipped by wind
and do not make a sound. They build in the eaves
one round, muddy nest after another until the house
is covered, and crap covers the windows, and they dart, silent
even as the hosed water loosens their nests and the stick
pries them off, they swoop and dive over the wreckage.

She closes her eyes
but not against sight.

Her sister's husband has died,
had the oldest boy help clean out the garage,
sent both kids off to camp, stuck a garden hose in the tailpipe.
Now she looks at the river pouring over its stones
and can't bear the motion, can't imagine the engine
diligently purring, what colors, what expressions

washed over his face, and why even grief now seems mechanical,
as does the river rolling over its bed.

The trout shudders and its impassive eye seems to blink,
or he thinks it's just the twitching of its head, as bloodless
it's slipped in the creel.

A storm cloud advances, rafting dark over the valley
then pelting it with rain, thunder which rumbles up from the river
into his legs. The air burns and shivers.
All is water around him, who does not move.

She stares out the window
at her melting husband.

Morning and the light is dusk's.
She weeps at the thought of her sister left, the children
with no father, the graceless helplessness of it,
that family across the continent in the emptying home.

He smells his hand for scent of the river.
Lifting it out of the creel to be cleaned, he looks over the trout,
the heft, the fading color of its stripe.
He sees one eye's blind, the one that would have faced him
when it was hooked.

In the kitchen, he tests the blade on his thumbnail.
Then she turns to look.

There are tears because the world's too beautiful here, as if beyond reach.
He walks again quietly behind her, puts his hand on her shoulder
and stares with her at the mountain, the river churning at its base.

She feels his hand is wet.

THE ROUNDS

Leaves pool around the maples' trunks,
orange, yellow, red. I see them

through a window and an opening
in the pine, three wooden legs

in pools of color. I believe
what I cannot see: the bare

branches lifting to a bluing sky,
a crow's loud cawing.

I know the leaves if left will brown
and die into the ground, come spring

return through roots and feed
the trees. Next year,

summer's sun will keep them green,
then waning light turn them orange,

yellow, red. The mysteries
have doors. These lakes of color,

these lit, lanced clouds, almost
the leap to faith.

> Of all the gods named,
> none calls.

> I walk the streets of a city,
> along the bank of a stream

> as if I had no face. I answer
> to a name, but it doesn't

> name me. Translated,
> the wind is my name.

I hear it now, lifting branches
as it runs through the trees.

My prayer is that if I speak,
the world is calling,

a body out of wind, waters.
If I cannot understand it,

I might read my way inside
as do the fingers of the blind.

I know what it is not to be seen
but not the invisible.

We look up, the telling glance
of our creature,

tip our eyes to the sky.
We climb past the lit air

of the globe, fly to the star-pocked
heavens, look down

at the blue marble of Earth,
and still crane our necks

in wonder. Come
the children, their eyes

open, curious, their hands
reaching, their small, quick feet.

All is mystery, uncommon
as the days are common,

one after one. What is it
we grow out of into this gray?

We learn to love this,
not that. Our lives

bring pain; what we don't
understand, we fear.

Come the children,
we come again to ourselves,

smile at the children's
smiles, we can almost

see ourselves, come light,
come dark.

    Fog lolls in the valley,
    whispering out the mouth,

    like the breath of ghosts,
    our sieved silence.

    We are the ground people,
    shrouded in clouds.

    When the white sky lowers,
    we hunker in our homes.

    Or is it now that the clouds
    rise out the ground,

    a fog of wet earth and cold air,
    our valley filled to the brim,

    our river cloaked, running white
    between banks, a white murmur.

    You there, looking down at us,
    if you are there,

    if you can believe our houses
    stand under this cloud,

    and our lives are lived inside
    this whiteness, do not imagine us

pale, muffled in our coats,
do not imagine us at all.

Back away from the hilltop
under your sky the other side.

We have our own imaginings.
When the cries of birds

rain down, we look up.
We would like to believe

the blue includes us, that day
and night include us,

that we walk the white
as well the blue, as creatures,

with the grace of animals,
part of the story, not the end.

Up above a vulture flies,
going nowhere, going on.

We stare at the broad, fixed
wings, the floating circles.

We see the hawk perched
on a pole, its stern eye.

No wonder we don't know
the way. It takes a voice

not ours to find it, a cry
that makes us stop, chilled,

though we can't say what
we've heard. The geese

cry as they sail overhead,
white with black-tipped wings.

Theirs is not a note like song
but a calling from the belly,

line after line shaping into Vs,
beating to take a place.

I look down at the cold, green water,
glance back up. I'd rather the birds

be kept by clouds, the calling
and beating wings stay hid,

the raucous chorus up above
whipped away by wind.

To see them, to wed flight and calling,
to see them beat as if a single wing,

their cries as if a sign ahead
that all might follow, followed,

is called to those behind
whose cries carry on,

as if their voice was the sky's itself,
and their flight its floating—nothing

our creature sings or says sounds
that round.

The mouth opens, a stutter comes.
Nothing calls us out the blue.

I listen, peering down at the green,
cold water, waves rocking the boat.

    The light falls everywhere, through rain,
    between and in the drops, down the slick

       dirt road, on the river's back.
       Even in the dark, the light falls,

in stars rubbed through night,
in the eyes that close and dream.

From the eaves, lines of water fall,
one and then another, never the same,

always perfectly straight. Water seams
stitch the world, these random drops, true

by gravity, falling, lifting the creeks.
The rain comes harder now,

and off the eaves fall clear, moving sheets.
Yesterday, as the clouds built, the birds

sang wildly. Today is just the sound
of water falling, one disappearing

curtain at a time. Inside the cabin,
music beats, and if you could see inside,

you'd find us tapping our feet, murmuring,
it would sound like song the things we say,

glancing into each other's eyes
only to meet another wall, these spaces

inside untouched by light, so dark I wonder
at her across the room, smiling,

and look behind myself to see if someone
else is there. Thus you see us,

by waters or on our knees, or on our knees
at the water, casting for hope.

All night I dream it, the line repeating:
the purpose of prayer is to assemble hope.

Outside, they're clearing the road
after the storm, sawing fallen limbs

and branches, piled onto tarps,
the tarps bound and heaved onto trucks.

No one knows where they go, some dump
or muddy landfill, but the piles look

like the burial mounds of an ancient people,
and the raked leaves could make

the exact puzzle of certain winds and rain
that howled like a beast of weather, cloaked

in its own gray clouds. If we saw it,
we'd shake our heads.

The beast would seem restful, even tender,
in need of care. We'd see

our discarded days, the hours spent without
wonder, the mountain of minutes distracted

from feeling, all the heartless waste
before it's plowed underground.

Last night, when the world seemed drowned,
I looked up. Through clouds, Orion shone

and I spoke to it, to stars so far away
and far apart, the distance shapes an image

of man. Only a human would look at long lost
light and believe. Only stars so far away

burn but do not blind the dark. And only
darkness brings us to our knees, and praying

for a night's black help, do we believe
in what we cannot see, the missing

heart in that stick-figure man, the beating
of our own red chests.

BENT to BREAKING

When the fish strikes, it seems as any
then races beyond control,
the reel screaming, unstoppable
as it swims with the current as if back to the sea.

Up on the bank, running after, the rod bent to break,
I see the breadth of its back and the fan of its tail,
twisting as it jumps and clears the river,
the white line in the water thinning to a thread.

In the campfire's ring of light, I sit in silence.
It's the time of night for stories, but I sit.

If only for moments, I touched something surging
with the will to survive. Then the line,
taut as if sewn to the surface, broke.
Still hooked, the fish was gone.
I stood, quietly shaking, eyes to a lowering sky.

The smoke shifts and the sting blinds.
I'm thinking of my wife, far away.
I'm entirely alive and thinking of the day I'm gone.
My hope is that our touches over the years
have found a way to say what bends words to break.
When I open my eyes, the fire's smoldering.
The sparks are like stars raining, up.

SLATE to GREEN

Dawn, and the sun breaks angled over the water;
a knot of cormorants fly as if hauling
the first light of day.

The day doubles as a window.
Out of red light, a white light settles, and the bay
turns slate to green.

It's early. Sleep.
Stripers roll, chasing bait to the surface.
The window's nothing more than the moment.
Only when you fall to one side do you see the frame.

Sleep. The sun has edges.
Its light will warm, now tinged with orange.
I'll be out there if you need me, out of reach,
surrounding like the sea.

OUT of SIGHT

Today, twice I had to stop casting and put down the rod.
The water shone and white clouds laced the blue.
A wave of geese came circling, the sky darkening
with the beats of their wings, filling with their cries,
anxious, as the flock rose higher and higher, then swirled
down out of sight.

Beauty like a satin fist.

Driving home, I pass an armchair dumped on the freeway,
the chair brown and somehow sad. My father's voice
weak on the phone, just a cold, he says, as he reminds me
of the anniversary of my mother's death. To this,
like a fool I reply that she's been on my mind. Tears brim,
not from sorrow but mirth, thinking of her, wishing
she'd lived long enough to come for a boat ride,
knowing she'd have agreed, stepped nervously on board,
and hated every minute.

SUNDAY BEST

Up from the water, coils of barbed wire glint in the sun,
the light off the bay against the walls of San Quentin,
and, from inside, the inmates' shouts rise up.

We cast toward shore, scratching at the shallows. The shouts
grow louder, and we wonder what's happening behind those walls,
those cries.

In the parking lot, families mill around their cars,
children, women, dim and overdressed, the men smoking, feet up
on bumpers or leaned against their trucks. One,

in an outsize cowboy hat, shouts as he sees a rod bend and the fish splash,
scrambles down the riprap to watch the fight. When we release it,
he shakes his head in disbelief, hands up, palms the same white of the walls.

FISHING REPORT

Driving down the levy,
the tules bent flat, the gulls
blown down to the chopped
water, dust whipped up
off the washboard ruts,

we stop and ask each
draped group hunkered
on the riprap, How's fishing?
and each shouts the same:
Wind's blowing!

FLOATING the MORNING

A sky with hot air balloons,
each gaudily colored, floating the morning
like upside down, marvelous tears,
but the luck's behind this old truck—

off the bumper, a leaky cooler drips.
Drop by drop, the water hangs like pearls,
by Angwin and the Seventh Day Adventists,
three balloons, four, five, six, and rose

hedges in bloom, mustard, yellow lakes of it,
the explosion, the second speed
of those drops when they hit the pavement
and vaporize like wishes.

Hands flicker in the vineyards.
Drip, vanish, drop, vanish, drip.
And the hubcap ranch, a half mile
of chrome eyes shining on barbed wire,

fog like a white breath, dew white as a beard,
that country wave, that little wag of just one finger,
as the old man turns off and I wave back,
water, wishes, the river in sight.

NOT FOR NOTHING

We open the chart and shine the light
on chance. We drift.

Over a hazardous dark,
the boat floats green inches.

We cast to what we can reach,
what the eye sees as promising, a guess

soon chastened, chasing something like faith.
Cast, searching

until the tide turns, and we turn
back to the deep, where we haven't a prayer.

Where we're safe, and the gulls circle.
Returning home with nothing, again.

And again will board, buckle the life vests.
Not for nothing, hunt.

PIECES

From the water to the sky.
On the water, the white stitches

of the high-flying swans.
In the air, the calls plaintive,

as if lost or weary of leaving,
and the wing-beats whistle,

or do I image that, down below,
seeing the ragged V reflected,

stitching another breaking wave.
The flock far off now

at the horizon's edge, the water
quiet, sewn to the sky.

THE SMALLEST PEACE

At the cliff-top clouds swarm,
and from gray shifts and folds
falls snow, covering paths to the river
where in summer I stalk its pools.

Now the low water chatters over rocks
and I can see each green quiet.
In the coldest season, hungry, I stare down
with nothing but yearnings unnamed,
yet the river gives, and with dry hands

I take it.
It seems now that the riffle's hiss is all
I've been wanting—this echo
swallowed as the next notes roll over stones,
this song whose canyon deepens but holds.

A quiet that keeps the smallest peace.
Snow falls like bits of words over the water,
and into the silence, each flake fits.

TO BE SURE

The fish a sickle shape,
as if caught

by ecstasy,
and lays shining

in quiet water.
One does this

to be sure,
pokes the stillness

with a stick.
Dead

quite some time
by the smell.

THE CIRCLING

The bald heads glare red
and the black wings stretch,
yet there's something lovely
in the circling vultures
lowering in the sky.

The darker the beauty
the more we're drawn.
It's not our words we hear
but our silence,
all we have almost said.

Death is just one word for it,
and puzzling's end.
While we're alive, questions
float over no answers.
Unsettling, isn't it,

when the black birds perch,
and tearing, begin to feed?
The dead deer twitches
with each bite.

INTO the NIGHT

Dark claims the depths, but the surface holds
the day's last light, a pale colorless hue
over the ridge top and pine spikes,

darker down the river's bend but still shining,
bats like bits of the coming dark, the rocks dim
as we wade into the river, feeling our way.

We're dim to each other except for the whistling
as we cast, guessing the distance to the murky,
opposite shore.

Cast and then step, cast and then step, and if we keep
casting, stepping downstream where it's utterly black,
will we keep between us a ripple of light?

If we keep at it all night, casting, wading downriver,
cold, stumbling, but coming up casting,
will we see finally where far and near merge,

that dark, that kernel where night grips the light?
Or will we stop, simply rise out the river, miles
from camp, blinded by dawn?

BLUE

Down the canyon, the train whistle
comes and goes like a melody sung,
forgotten, then hummed.

Coming down the crest, views of the valley open,
veins of green that follow the creeks that feed
the river, the largest one named Ruby.

What we've lost matters so little, it makes
the time spent in grief or anger a waste,
which makes us grieve again.

And so it weighs, and we cannot find our way,
even in dreams, in a smile so sweet
it makes us happy when we wake.

There is the other wake. And what
a boat leaves as the oars dip beneath the surface
and lift, dripping with water.

Lost and hopeless, we decide we are alone.
Yet, all the tears braid in the current
into one luscious blue.

NEW WATER

Always singly and far apart, deer prints,
as if a doe had landed on just one hoof
then bounded up. The sky pewter, crumbling,
the dense woods sewn with brambles, path broken,
heaved. Pushing

the mind into the body, trying to outrun it,
legs, breath, aching through the trees. Losing track
of the trails' twists, forks, toward it—
what we call the woods but mean the strange, the dark
but say haunted—lost,

I grow afraid, then ashamed. Push on
past every creaking tree, each weighted step toward
new water. As if some promise lies in the metal flavor
on the tongue, sweat stinging. Between the gasps,
whistling wind.

The river barely moving, leaves caught on the surface
floating quietly away. Not a bird in the branches,
not a swish of fin, not a whisper, just dirty water, brown
with mud, choked with its own slow dredging.
Way too deep to cross.

SUN UP

Dawn, and the mountain brightens, its dark dropping inch by inch
as the sun rises and lights the cliffs and trees, the line
of etched shadow slowly slipping in the river between, then
up the opposite range, the water black then green, then back again.

Make of it what you will.

Days we stand alone, or believe the dimming, the light,
the kingfisher chattering as it leaves it branch, the osprey silent,
eagle coasting, wingspan for an instant shading the sun.

Make do.

I come down to the river like a bear for a drink but I am not thirsty.
There's a hunger in my heart that has no name, for all its darkness,
loves the light. Huge salmon, bronze-colored, leap out of the river
as they swim upstream. Up to my knees and the water cold,
current pressing. Step and step again, up to my chest.
Sun up, I stumble. Morning, I stumble. Afternoon, dusk I fall.

THE DEER

The mountain green with trees, shaped like a child's drawing,
an upside down V that notches the earth.

The sky spills violet on the river, the one thing the current can't carry away.
The world turns its face.

In the town, faces of women, all ages, always it's to the women I look,
as if there's a beauty yet to touch.

There's the woman I love, far away, like the deer disappearing into the woods,
the patch of black it leaves behind.

The moon's up, etching the valley with light, and now, though it's fool's gold,
everyone sees the moonlight's path rest at their feet.

Under their caps, the men's faces darken. At last light, steps churning,
we wade to the bank,

moving in a slow procession, looking down to the next dark step,
and, of course, glancing back.

Weary, we're fishless, to the one, wet and dim. I see that I might be able
to give more, all ways.

SOMETHING to CHERISH

And that day when the river's far
and only the freeway to thank for a sound
like water rushing?
At the edge of town, clouds lower,
mayflies begin to hatch.
I open the car door, look for my wallet.
Something was lost last night, I can feel it.
Wind rakes the leaves on the street.
Swallows dart above the river,
swooping down, gliding up, insect wings
sticking out their beaks.
It might be that I'm on a stream
or sitting on the front steps of my house,
rushing through a life that might be my own
but I'm too much in a hurry to notice.
Always the birds, the flock of starlings
wheeling, the cries of a circling hawk.
I stop.
The river teaches time, its endless change,
its long geology, the riffles quick.
The water tells you where to go.
Slow down.
She found a small feather on the bank,
goose, she thought, and made me a gift.
In the distance, the ocean,
I can almost hear the waves.
And one day I'll walk home
with the same sure steps I use leaving the river.
She'll sit down beside me and smile.
She'll have a glass of wine or nothing.
What difference does it make?
There's her brown eyes, sure as the light.
If I open mine, I can see my life,
candid as a dream, something to cherish.
The sun's going down, the best time
to be on a river. Open the door.

About the Author

Keith Shein is the author of six books of poetry and is the recipient of grants and awards. He's a graduate of the writing program at San Francisco State University, has served as the poetry critic for the San Francisco Examiner newspaper, and has directed poetry reading series in the Bay Area. His work has appeared in magazines, anthologies and on-line forums.

Made in the USA
San Bernardino, CA
09 July 2015